The Pa

Written by R
Illustrated by

The frying pan,

the flour,

the eggs,

the milk,

the butter,

the pancake.

9

The pancake race!

Talk about the story

Spot the difference

Find the five differences in the two pictures.

Floppy Floppy

Written by Roderick Hunt
Illustrated by Alex Brychta

Oh, Floppy!

No, Floppy!

Oh, Floppy!

No, Floppy!

Floppy Floppy.

Talk about the story

Match the shadows

Can you match the pictures of Floppy with the shadows of Floppy?